BLESSINGS

15 WORSHIPFUL FAVORITES ARRANGED BY PHILLIP KEVEREN

— PIANO LEVEL —
LATE INTERMEDIATE/EARLY ADVANCED

ISBN 978-1-4950-5901-8

HAL•LEONARD®
CORPORATION
7777 W. BLUEMOUND RD. P.O. BOX 13819 MILWAUKEE, WI 53213

Visit Hal Leonard Online at
www.halleonard.com

Visit Phillip at
www.phillipkeveren.com

PREFACE

This collection of piano solos brings together recent Contemporary Christian songs with classics from earlier eras. Whether from the last ten years or past century, each of these songs has been a vital part of the music of the church.

"Blessings" is a composition of extraordinary beauty from the pen of Laura Story (2011). "Great Is Thy Faithfulness" remains one of the most beloved hymns from the 20th century (1923). A personal favorite of mine, "You Are My All in All" (1991), makes a wonderful solo for the piano.

May these settings be a blessing to you!

Sincerely,
Phillip Keveren

Phillip Keveren

BIOGRAPHY

Phillip Keveren, a multi-talented keyboard artist and composer, has composed original works in a variety of genres from piano solo to symphonic orchestra. Mr. Keveren gives frequent concerts and workshops for teachers and their students in the United States, Canada, Europe, and Asia. Mr. Keveren holds a B.M. in composition from California State University Northridge and a M.M. in composition from the University of Southern California.

CONTENTS

BECAUSE HE LIVES, AMEN

Words and Music by WILLIAM J. GAITHER,
GLORIA GAITHER, DANIEL CARSON,
CHRIS TOMLIN, ED CASH, MATT MAHER
and JASON INGRAM
Arranged by Phillip Keveren

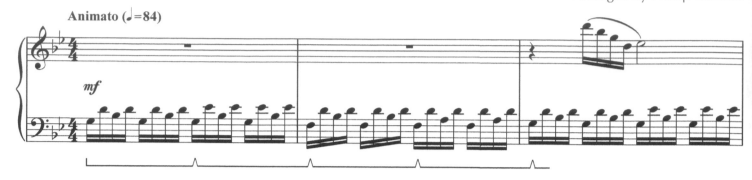

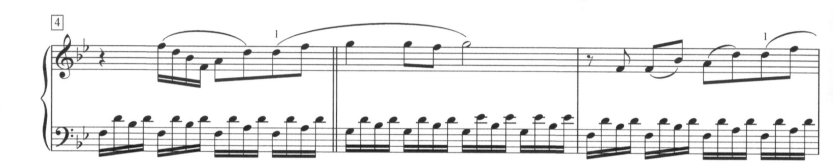

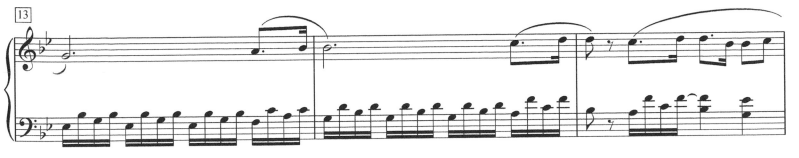

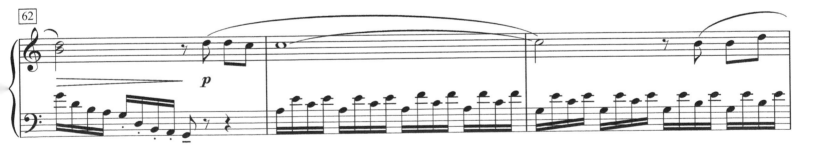

BLESSED BE YOUR NAME

Words and Music by MATT REDMAN
and BETH REDMAN
Arranged by Phillip Keveren

Flowing (♩ = 116)

BLESSINGS

Words and Music by
LAURA MIXON STORY
Arranged by Phillip Keveren

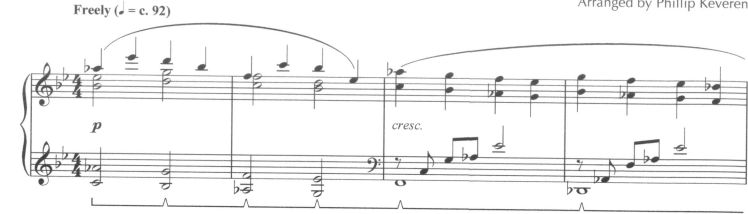

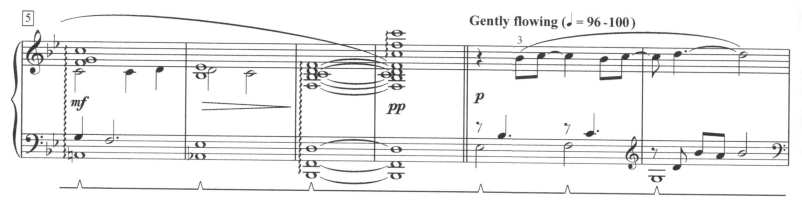

14

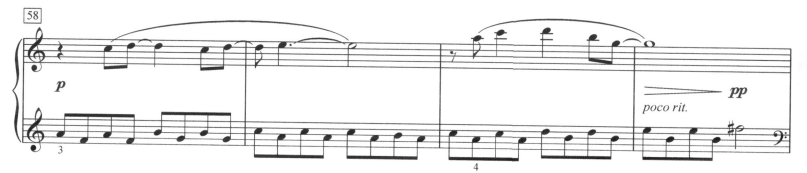

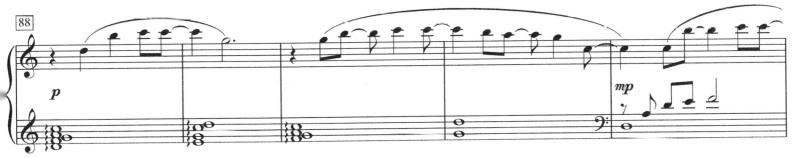

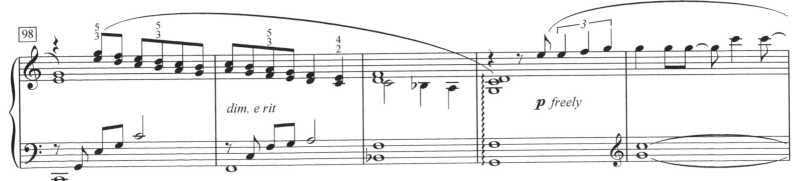

CORNERSTONE

Words and Music by JONAS MYRIN,
REUBEN MORGAN, ERIC LILJERO
and EDWARD MOTE
Arranged by Phillip Keveren

Rubato (♩ = c. 80)

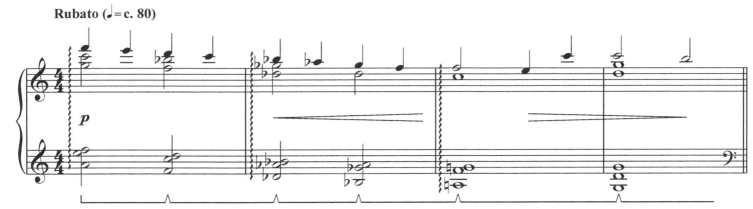

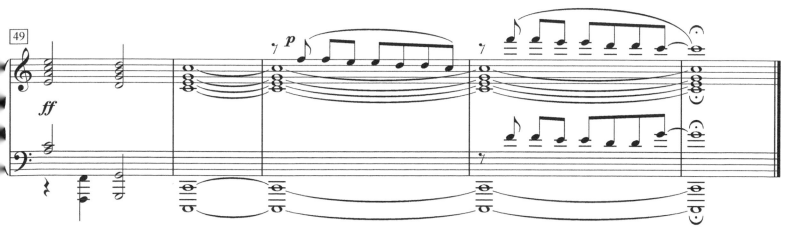

BROKEN VESSELS
(Amazing Grace)

Words and Music by JOEL HOUSTON
and JONAS MYRIN
Arranged by Phillip Keveren

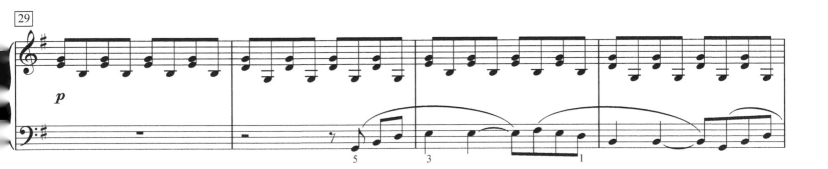

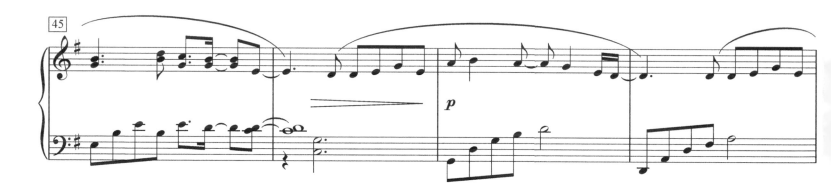

GOOD GOOD FATHER

Words and Music by PAT BARRETT
and ANTHONY BROWN
Arranged by Phillip Keveren

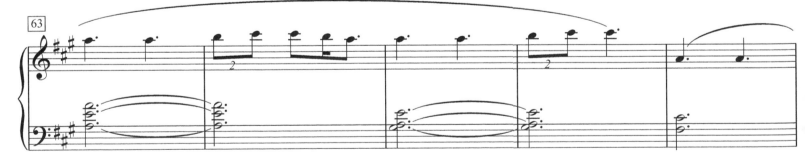

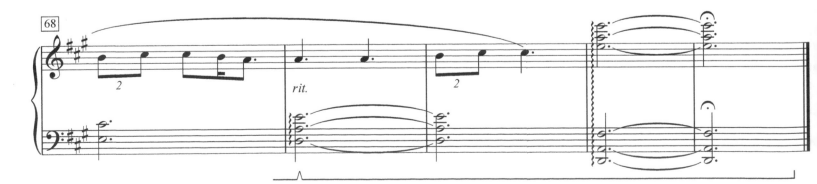

GREAT IS THY FAITHFULNESS

Words by THOMAS O. CHISHOLM
Music by WILLIAM M. RUNYAN
Arranged by Phillip Keveren

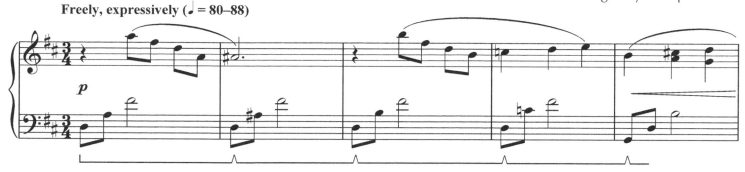

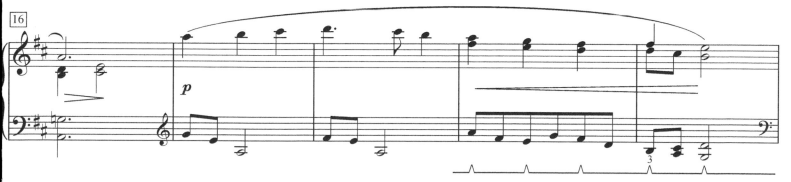

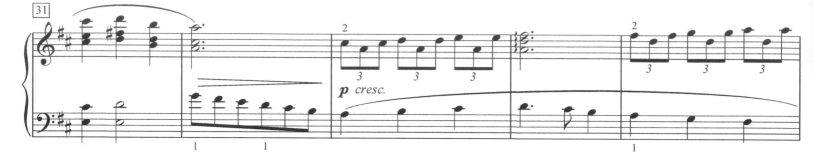

HOLY SPIRIT

Words and Music by KATIE TORWALT
and BRYAN TORWALT
Arranged by Phillip Keveren

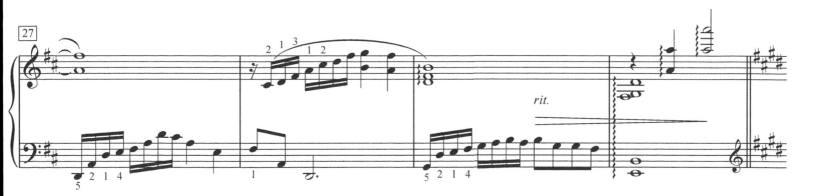

THIS IS AMAZING GRACE

Words and Music by PHIL WICKHAM,
JOSHUA NEIL FARRO and JEREMY RIDDLE
Arranged by Phillip Keveren

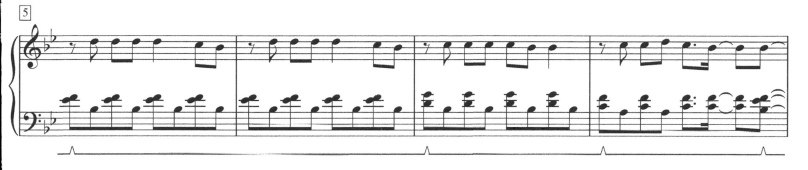

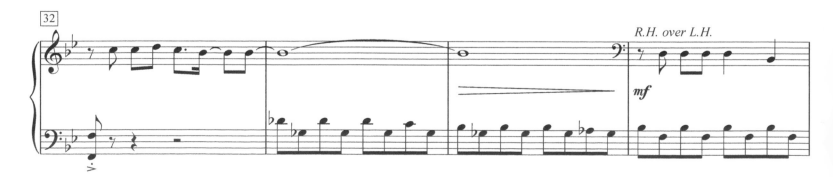

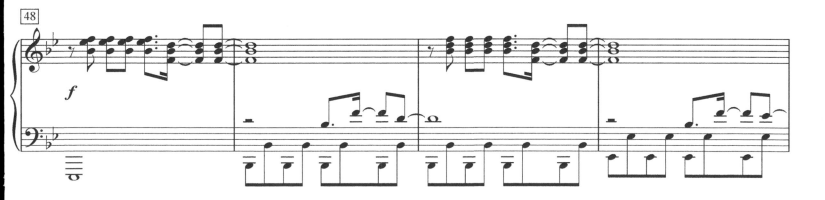

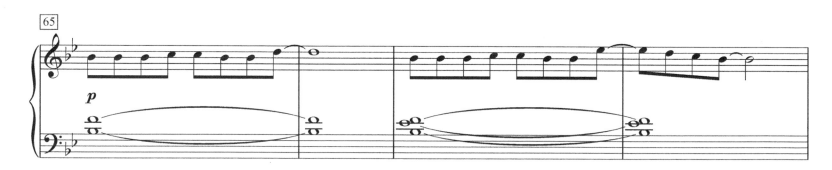

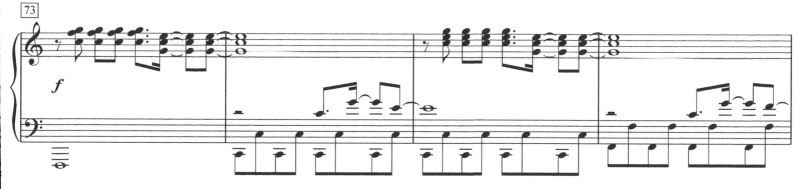

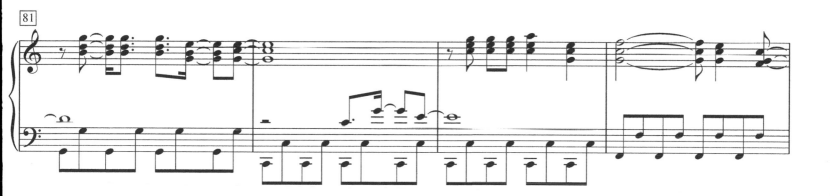

HOW DEEP THE FATHER'S LOVE FOR US

Words and Music by
STUART TOWNEND
Arranged by Phillip Keveren

WE BELIEVE

Words and Music by TRAVIS RYAN,
MATTHEW HOOPER and RICHIE FIKE
Arranged by Phillip Keveren

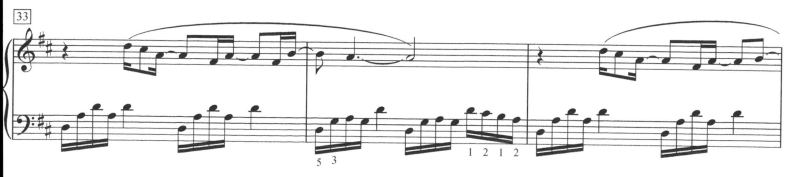

YOUR GREAT NAME

Words and Music by MICHAEL NEALE
and KRISSY NORDHOFF

Expressively (♩ = 76)

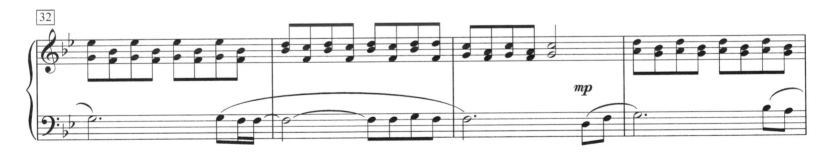

WHOM SHALL I FEAR
(God of Angel Armies)

Words and Music by CHRIS TOMLIN,
ED CASH and SCOTT CASH

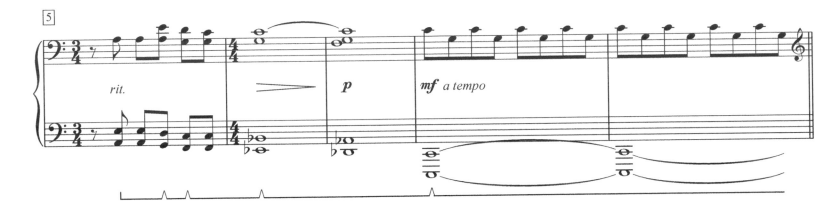

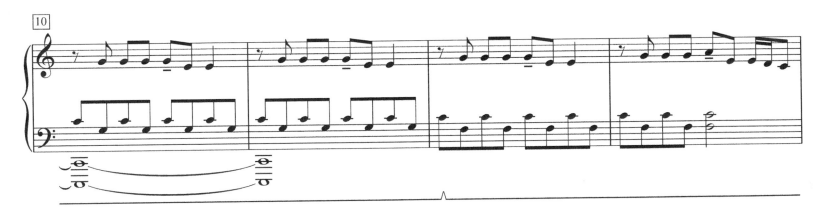

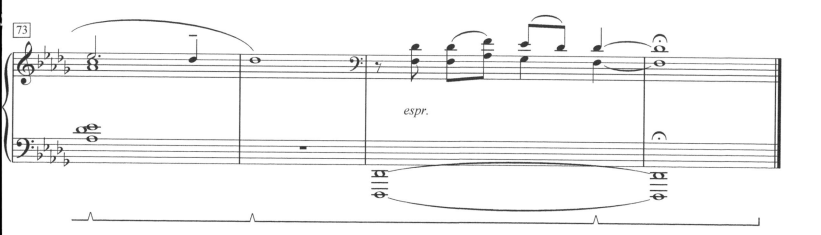

YOU ARE MY ALL IN ALL

By DENNIS JERNIGAN
Arranged by Phillip Keveren

53

YOUR NAME

Words and Music by PAUL BALOCHE
and GLENN PACKIAM
Arranged by Phillip Keveren

THE PHILLIP KEVEREN SERIES

PIANO SOLO

ABBA FOR CLASSICAL PIANO
00156644......$14.99

ABOVE ALL
00311024......$12.99

BACH MEETS JAZZ
00198473......$14.99

THE BEATLES
00306412......$16.99

THE BEATLES FOR CLASSICAL PIANO
00312189......$14.99

THE BEATLES – RECITAL SUITES
00275876......$19.99

BEST PIANO SOLOS
00312546......$14.99

BLESSINGS
00156601......$12.99

BLUES CLASSICS
00198656......$12.99

BROADWAY'S BEST
00310669......$14.99

A CELTIC CHRISTMAS
00310629......$12.99

THE CELTIC COLLECTION
00310549......$12.95

CELTIC SONGS WITH A CLASSICAL FLAIR
00280571......$12.99

CHRISTMAS MEDLEYS
00311414......$12.99

CHRISTMAS AT THE MOVIES
00312190......$14.99

CHRISTMAS SONGS FOR CLASSICAL PIANO
00233788......$12.99

CINEMA CLASSICS
00310607......$14.99

CLASSICAL JAZZ
00311083......$12.95

COLDPLAY FOR CLASSICAL PIANO
00137779......$15.99

DISNEY RECITAL SUITES
00249097......$16.99

DISNEY SONGS FOR CLASSICAL PIANO
00311754......$16.99

DISNEY SONGS FOR RAGTIME PIANO
00241379......$16.99

THE FILM SCORE COLLECTION
00311811......$14.99

FOLKSONGS WITH A CLASSICAL FLAIR
00269408......$12.99

GOLDEN SCORES
00233789......$14.99

GOSPEL GREATS
00144351......$12.99

GREAT STANDARDS
00311157......$12.95

THE HYMN COLLECTION
00311071......$12.99

HYMN MEDLEYS
00311349......$12.99

HYMNS IN A CELTIC STYLE
00280705......$12.99

HYMNS WITH A CLASSICAL FLAIR
00269407......$12.99

HYMNS WITH A TOUCH OF JAZZ
00311249......$12.99

JINGLE JAZZ
00310762......$14.99

BILLY JOEL FOR CLASSICAL PIANO
00175310......$15.99

ELTON JOHN FOR CLASSICAL PIANO
00126449......$15.99

LET FREEDOM RING!
00310839......$12.99

ANDREW LLOYD WEBBER
00313227......$15.99

MANCINI MAGIC
00313523......$14.99

MORE DISNEY SONGS FOR CLASSICAL PIANO
00312113......$15.99

MOTOWN HITS
00311295......$12.95

PIAZZOLLA TANGOS
00306870......$15.99

QUEEN FOR CLASSICAL PIANO
00156645......$15.99

RICHARD RODGERS CLASSICS
00310755......$15.99

SHOUT TO THE LORD!
00310699......$14.99

SONGS FROM CHILDHOOD FOR EASY CLASSICAL PIANO
00233688......$12.99

THE SOUND OF MUSIC
00119403......$14.99

SYMPHONIC HYMNS FOR PIANO
00224738......$14.99

TIN PAN ALLEY
00279673......$12.99

TREASURED HYMNS FOR CLASSICAL PIANO
00312112......$14.99

THE TWELVE KEYS OF CHRISTMAS
00144926......$12.99

YULETIDE JAZZ
00311911......$17.99

EASY PIANO

AFRICAN-AMERICAN SPIRITUALS
00310610......$10.99

CATCHY SONGS FOR PIANO
00218387......$12.99

CELTIC DREAMS
00310973......$10.95

CHRISTMAS CAROLS FOR EASY CLASSICAL PIANO
00233686......$12.99

CHRISTMAS POPS
00311126......$14.99

CLASSIC POP/ROCK HITS
00311548......$12.95

A CLASSICAL CHRISTMAS
00310769......$10.95

CLASSICAL MOVIE THEMES
00310975......$12.99

CONTEMPORARY WORSHIP FAVORITES
00311805......$14.99

DISNEY SONGS FOR EASY CLASSICAL PIANO
00144352......$12.99

EARLY ROCK 'N' ROLL
00311093......$12.99

GEORGE GERSHWIN CLASSICS
00110374......$12.99

GOSPEL TREASURES
00310805......$12.99

THE VINCE GUARALDI COLLECTION
00306821......$16.99

HYMNS FOR EASY CLASSICAL PIANO
00160294......$12.99

IMMORTAL HYMNS
00310798......$12.99

JAZZ STANDARDS
00311294......$12.99

LOVE SONGS
00310744......$12.99

THE MOST BEAUTIFUL SONGS FOR EASY CLASSICAL PIANO
00233740......$12.99

POP STANDARDS FOR EASY CLASSICAL PIANO
00233739......$12.99

RAGTIME CLASSICS
00311293......$10.95

SONGS FROM CHILDHOOD FOR EASY CLASSICAL PIANO
00233688......$12.99

SONGS OF INSPIRATION
00103258......$12.99

TIMELESS PRAISE
00310712......$12.95

10,000 REASONS
00126450......$14.99

TV THEMES
00311086......$12.99

21 GREAT CLASSICS
00310717......$12.99

WEEKLY WORSHIP
00145342......$16.99

BIG-NOTE PIANO

CHILDREN'S FAVORITE MOVIE SONGS
00310838......$12.99

CHRISTMAS MUSIC
00311247......$10.95

CLASSICAL FAVORITES
00277368......$12.99

CONTEMPORARY HITS
00310907......$12.99

DISNEY FAVORITES
00277370......$14.99

JOY TO THE WORLD
00310888......$10.95

THE NUTCRACKER
00310908......$10.99

STAR WARS
00277371......$16.99

BEGINNING PIANO SOLOS

AWESOME GOD
00311202......$12.99

CHRISTIAN CHILDREN'S FAVORITES
00310837......$12.99

CHRISTMAS FAVORITES
00311246......$10.95

CHRISTMAS TIME IS HERE
00311334......$12.99

CHRISTMAS TRADITIONS
00311117......$10.99

EASY HYMNS
00311250......$12.99

EVERLASTING GOD
00102710......$10.99

JAZZY TUNES
00311403......$10.95

PIANO DUET

CLASSICAL THEME DUETS
00311350......$10.99

HYMN DUETS
00311544......$12.99

PRAISE & WORSHIP DUETS
00311203......$12.99

STAR WARS
00119405......$14.99

WORSHIP SONGS FOR TWO
00253545......$12.99

HAL•LEONARD®

Visit **www.halleonard.com**
for a complete series listing.

Prices, contents, and availability subject to change without notice.